BIG
HAIRY
MAD®

WARNER BOOKS

A Warner Communications Company

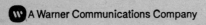

In the old days, kids would look up to "Groups" ...like the New York Yankees or the Green Bay Packers ... strong, skilled athletes who would set shining examples for the Youth of America to emulate. Later generations would idolize "Rock" Groups ... like the Beatles or the Rolling Stones ... funny-looking guys, yes, but at least they could sing. Today's kids are looking up to and emulating an entirely different kind of Group. This Group barfs, spits up, guzzles beer, molests women, flunks tests and holds orgies. Evidently, America's Youth feels this is lots more fun than playing ball or singing. We mean the Group from ...

ABOMINAL HOUSE

ARTIST: MORT DRUCKER   WRITER: ARNIE KOGEN   ADDITIONAL DIALOGUE: DICK DE BARTOLO

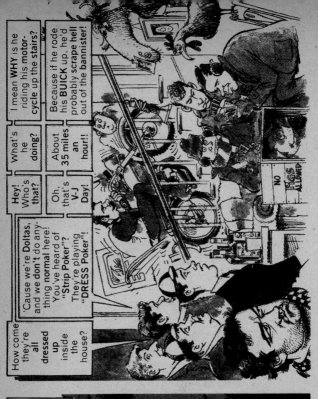

Not NOW! Not while I'm running away with this picture! I don't need him around to start stealing scenes!

AAAAAGHHHHH!

No! Not him! I don't want HIM here!

The kid's okay!

Yeah!

Alright! Krocker is in! How about this next pledgee?

Listen, guys... we just can't keep on rejecting pledgees by throwing things at the movie screen!

No... we're running out of movie screens!

Why? Are we running out of pledgees...?

Now this next guy is Leery Krocker! Any comments...?

I've come to this hell-hole of a fraternity to set you creeps straight! You clowns are the scum of the campus! Your house grade-point average is a disgrace, the lowest in Farber history! And your behavior... your drinking and carousing could get you expelled! Now, what do you plan to do about it?

We plan to throw a "Toga Party"... raise hell... and seduce your wife!

Good! As long as we understand each other!

Tell me, what exactly IS a "Toga Party" anyway?

It gives us a chance to put on sheets and go berserk!

Y'know, there's another bunch of guys into that!

Another frat... here on campus?

No, the Ku Klux Klan!

Right! But I don't think they'd hire the same band!

SHOUT — A LITTLE BIT SOFTER NOW! SHOUT — A LITTLE BIT LOUDER NOW! SHOUT — A LITTLE BIT REPETITIOUS NOW! SHOUT — A LITTLE BIT BORING NOW! SHOUT — IT'S SO NOISY NOW!

I'm—I'm sorry about all this TISSUE PAPER, Leery . . .
Oh, I understand! You have to pack those things very carefully so they don't break while you're dancing!

The meeting of the Pan-Hellraising Disciplinary Committee will come to order! Proceed directly with the charges against—*yech*—Dolta House!
It is charged that Dolta House members are guilty of the following disgusting, perverted and obscene acts!
1. Conducting a lewd Toga Party! 2. Having intimate relations with a minor! 3. Having intimate relations with a chicken!
4. Roller skating on a virgin! 5. Dancing the twist on the Mayor's face!
6. Opening an umbrella inside a campus Policeman's pants! 7. Finger-painting a Pom-Pom Girl!
Hey . . . no one's perfect! So I painted outside the lines!!
STUDENT COURT
COLLEG

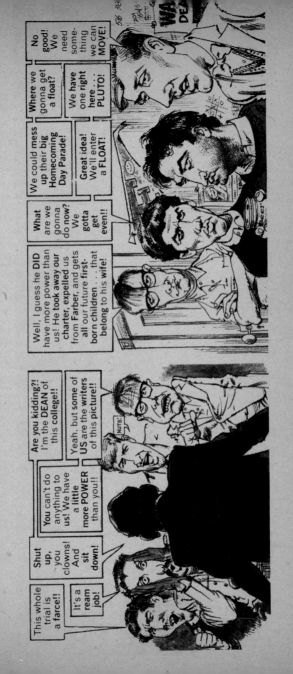

Dean Wormy, look!! Where did that ridiculous CAKE float come from?!
Oh, it was probably entered by one of our GAY frats—OH! NO!
It's those clowns from DOLTA HOUSE! They're trying to destroy our parade . . .!!
MOXIE'S
ΔTX
And I think they're SUCCEEDING!!
Just look at those college kids . . . smoking pot, driving recklessly, having no respect for anything! What can that possible train them for?
DEATHMOBILE
A career in Government Service!

VINCENT JAMES DAY '63

Legal Assistant to
Ralph Nader.

ROBERT HOOVERVAC '63

Had Sex-Change Operation. Now
A Leading Female Tennis Pro.

KINK BARFMAN '66

Missing Since 1971. Rumored To
Have Been Sucked Into A Tuba.

G. BRENT MARMALADE '63

Rabbi —Temple B'nai Loaded
Rockville Centre, New York.

DIRK NEITCHEMEYER '63

Successful Stand-up Comedian
Hollywood, California.

DEAN VERNAL WORMY '48

Burned At Stake During Student
Demonstations. Berkeley. 1967.

MRS. WORMY 38-27-38

Arrested For Molesting A Minor
Now Serving 10-20. Chattahoochee.

JOHN MOP PLUTO '63

Advisor to Pres. Nixon '68-'72
Advisor to Pres. Ford '73-'74
Advisor to Pres. Carter '74—

EARLY ONE MORNING IN SOUTH AMERICA

THE LIGHTER

SURP

SIDE OF...

RISES

ARTIST & WRITER:
DAVE BERG

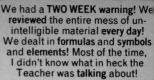

Darn it! We had a surprise test in **Chemistry** today!

I **hate** when Teachers pull sneaky things like that! They must have **sadistic streaks!** The least they could do is give a little **warning!**

We had a **TWO WEEK** warning! We **reviewed** the entire mess of un-intelligible material **every day!** We dealt in **formulas** and **symbols** and **elements!** Most of the time, I didn't know what in heck the Teacher was **talking** about!

And every night, I sweated over **homework** on the same impossible subject matter!

So **why** do you call it a **"surprise test"?!?**

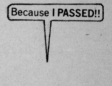

Because **I PASSED!!**

YAAH!

You scared the **heck** out of me! **Look** at me! I'm **shaking** like a **leaf!!**

You **poor man!** Let me get you a **shot** of **whiskey** to **calm** you **down!** After all, it isn't **every** day we get the **Super** up here to make **repairs!**

WHAT Super?! **WHAT** repairs?! I was **robbing** your **apartment!**

HA-HA!! That was **hilarious!** The **look of surprise** on your face was **absolutely priceless!**

But all kidding aside, this is the **REAL Peanut Brittle** I made for you! Tell me how you **like** it!

YECCH! I'd **rather** have the can of **snakes!!**

ONE EVENING IN A GEORGIA BUS TERMINAL

CROCK-IN-SPIELS DEPT.

A MAD
LOOK AT...

HALF TRUTHS
IN TV ADS

ARTIST: AL JAFFEE   WRITER: PAUL PETER PORGES

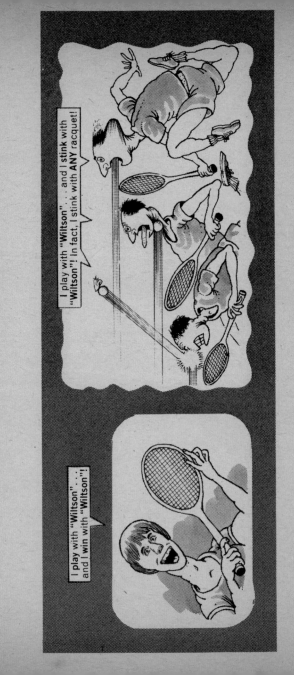

I was nervous and edgy until I tried Stanka Decaffinated Coffee . . .
Now, I'm nervous and edgy because I'm always late from over-sleeping!
SURGICAL APPOINTMENTS
9:00AM $1000
9:15AM $1200
9:25AM $9000
9:35AM $1600
10:00AM $2800
11:21
CHARGE!
AMA

. . . and your friendly Homeowners Protective Man is right on the spot to help . . .
HPI
That's about fifty dollars for the fence . . . and seventy-five dollars for the window! Which doesn't quite make the two hundred dollar deductible . . .!

Modern science has come up with a fantastic new gimmick: a strip of paper . . . chemically treated so when you rub it with your fingernail, an aroma is released. These so-called "Scratch 'n' Sniff" strips are being used by perfume makers to provide samples of their products, and by publishers to create scented books and magazines. Now people who've lived in Kansas all their lives can experience the smell of the ocean, city dwellers can enjoy the fragrance of a cow pasture, and millions of men can thrill to the erotic odor of Farrah Fawcett's armpit without even dating her. We here at MAD are so excited over this big scientific development that we have gone to great effort and expense to imprint these 3 pages with various aromas so that we can share with our readers the thrill of this great invention. Herewith is a selection of

MAD

"SCRATCH 'N' SNIFF" STRIPS

TO THOROUGHLY ENJOY STRIPS ✱ SCRAPE THE BLACK RECTANGLES FIRMLY WITH YOUR FINGERNAIL ✱ HOLD PAGE APPROXIMATELY 3 to 4 INCHES FROM NOSE ✱ INHALE DEEPLY

SCRATCH 'N' SNIFF
for a soothing aromatic sniff of
SAFE CIGARETTE SMOKE

SCRATCH 'N' SNIFF
for the wholesome, invigorating smell of
CLEAN CITY AIR

SCRATCH 'N' SNIFF
for the delectable aroma of preservative-free, chemical-free and artificial ingredient-free
HOME COOKING

SCRATCH 'N' SNIFF
for the tangy odor of
FRESH PAINT
from a Slumlord tenement

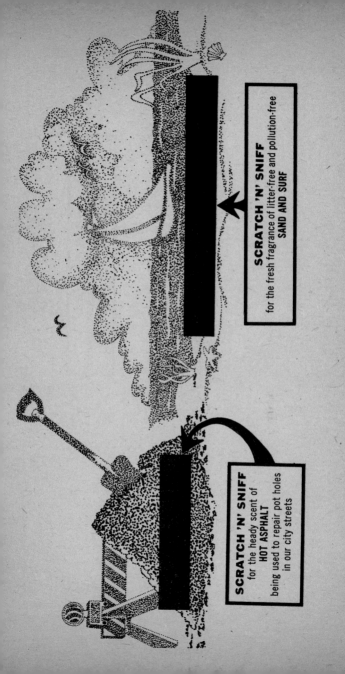

SCRATCH 'N' SNIFF
for the heady scent of
HOT ASPHALT
being used to repair pot holes
in our city streets

SCRATCH 'N' SNIFF
for the fresh fragrance of litter-free and pollution-free
SAND AND SURF

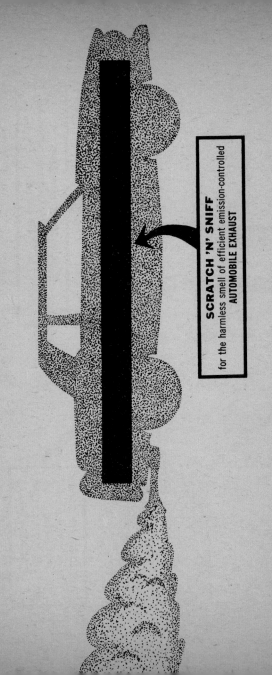

SCRATCH 'N' SNIFF
for the harmless smell of efficient emission-controlled
AUTOMOBILE EXHAUST

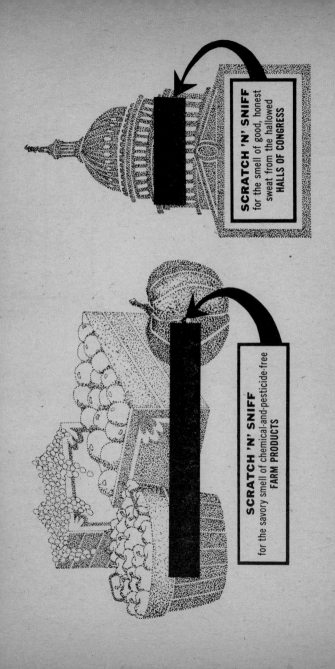

SCRATCH 'N' SNIFF for the smell of good, honest sweat from the hallowed **HALLS OF CONGRESS**

SCRATCH 'N' SNIFF for the savory smell of chemical-and-pesticide-free **FARM PRODUCTS**

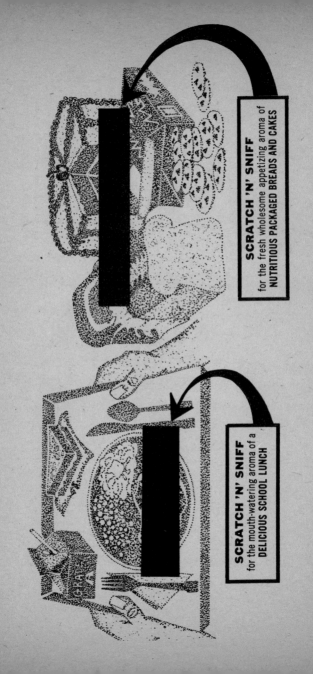

SCRATCH 'N' SNIFF
for the fresh wholesome appetizing aroma of
NUTRITIOUS PACKAGED BREADS AND CAKES

SCRATCH 'N' SNIFF
for the mouth-watering aroma of a
DELICIOUS SCHOOL LUNCH

MAD

THE UNITED STATES OF AM

THE FEDERAL RESERVE NOT

THIS IS NOT LEGAL TENDER
FOR ALL DEBTS, PUBLIC AND PRIVATE

B 50
w

B75276685C
2

SCRATCH 'N' SNIFF
for the mint-clean smell of a
brand new inflation-free
DOLLAR BILL

OOOOOPS!!!

It seemed like a good idea at the
time, but MAD's Research Department
tried and tried...and it just
couldn't come up with even a small
sample of any of these smells! We
are running the article anyway, be—
cause we had to fill up the space!
But even if you scratch your finger
to the bone and inhale so deeply
you get a nosebleed you ain't
gonna smell a thing!

Sorry about that!

THE EDITORS

DIDJA EVER NOTICE THAT...

ARTIST: BOB JONES   WRITER: LOU SILVERSTONE

Policemen and Firemen who go out on strike without any regard for the Public Safety . . .

. . . suddenly become very concerned about the people's health and well-being when they're faced with cost-cutting layoffs.

Law and Order lovers who scream whenever a Cop is shot . . .

. . . continue to fight against Gun Control Legislation, even though Cops are usually the victims of gun-toting maniacs.

Politicians who scream "Preserve the Law!" the loudest . . .

. . . are usually the ones who are discovered breaking it.

Some of the people who are opposed to abortion because they believe that everybody has a right to life . . .

. . . are gung ho about bombing and killing anyone that they consider to be a threat to our form of Democracy.

Some of the very same people who preach patriotism and liberty and the flag and the Constitution . . .

. . . think it's perfectly okay for the CIA to spy on Americans.

Many of the alleged Liberals who demand school busing . . .

. . send their own kids to lily-white private schools.

Mothers who scream loudest when someone picks on their kids . . .

. . . manage to look the other way when their brat starts clobbering some smaller child.

Those "Winning is everything!" Coaches who engage in underhanded recruiting with no regard for the future of their players are honored by their Universities . . .

. . . but a Coach who recruits according to the rules and thinks it's important that his players do well in school-work is fired because his team doesn't make the Top Ten.

City-dwellers who moved out to the suburbs so they would have clean air to breathe . . .

. . . are doing their damndest to pollute it with wood-burning fireplaces and daily barbecue cookouts and Fall leaf-burning.

nce, like us, you're probably up to here with
ose tiresome candid snapshots of "Great
oments in Sports", we now present—

MAD'S
Candid
Snapshots Of
Some
Insignificant
Moments
n Sports

T & WRITER: PAUL PETER PORGES

SIMPLE POP FLY DURING SING SING
ANNUAL INTERMURAL BASEBALL GAME

ED START OF INTERNATIONAL WATER POLC

ONE-MAN SCRAMBLE FOR FOUL BALL DURING
LATE SEASON BLUE JAYS—MARINERS GAME

GOLF PRO IN ROUGH DURING AMAZON OPEN

U.S. BOBSLED TEAM TAKING A COFFEE BREAK

DISTRACTED NET JUDGE DURING FINALS AT THE WARSAW LAWN TENNIS INVITATIONALS

RELEASE OF PIGEONS AT CEREMONY OPENING THE XVIII OLYMPIC GAMES

FANS DISAGREEING WITH REFEREE'S CALL
SOUTH AMERICAN SOCCER CHAMPIONSHIP

BANTAMWEIGHT CONTENDER MISTAKINGLY USING HEAVYWEIGHT'S MOUTHPIECE AT GOLDEN GLOVES

BIG UPSET DURING ANNUAL OKEFENOKEE SWAMP GATOR-WRESTLING CHAMPIONSHIP

DELAYED CALL GIANTS-DOLPHINS COIN TOSS

INTRODUCTION OF ICE HOCKEY'S OLD TIMERS

IT MAY BE DIFFICULT TO BELIEVE, SINCE NONE OF US SEEM TO HOLD ON TO IT LONG ENOUGH TO STRIKE UP A CONVERSATION WITH, BUT

MONEY TALKS

ARTIST: BOB CLARKE   WRITER: HENRY CLARK

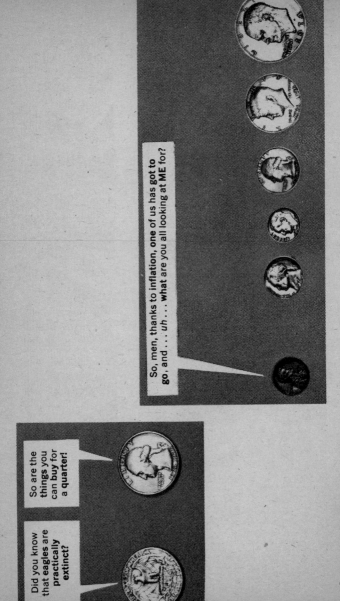

Coin collectors have the right idea! If you hold on to a coin long enough, its value will double!
Yes, but in the meantime, the prices of things will have tripled!

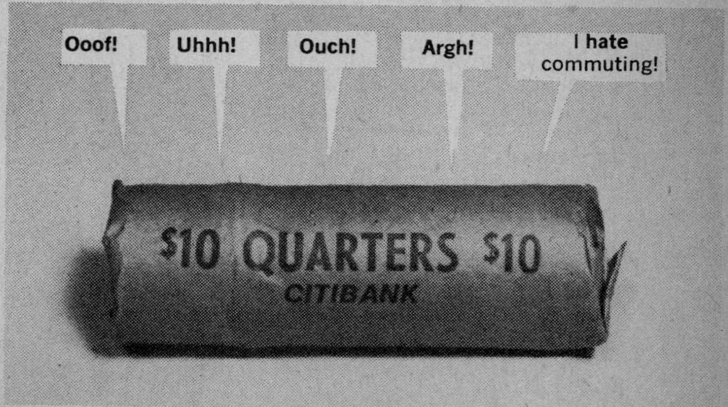
Ooof!
Uhhh!
Ouch!
Argh!
I hate commuting!
$10 QUARTERS $10
CITIBANK

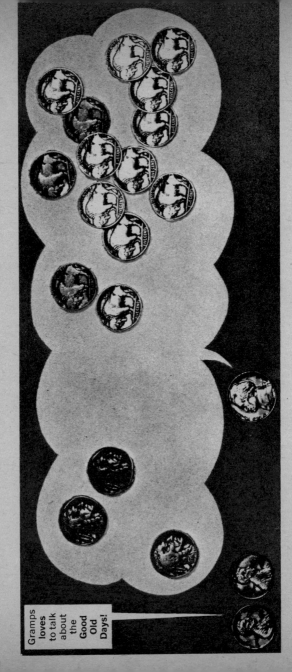

Gramps loves to talk about the **Good Old Days!**

Remember the terrific "Mary Tyler Moore Show" of a couple of seasons back? It took place in the newsroom of a mythical TV station, where a funny Editor and his funny Staff got involved in a different funny story every week. Well, that Editor now has a TV show of his own where he plays a similar role as the City Editor of a mythical newspaper. The only difference is that now he's no longer surrounded by a funny Staff . . . and the stories he gets involved in every week aren't very funny either. Which may help to explain why he's now known as . . .

Lou Grouch

ARTIST: ANGELO TORRES   WRITER: TOM KOCH

I'm sure City Hall is ordering those small fires set, just to get more money for the Fire Department! So let's go tell Mrs. Pynchbottom, our Publisher, how we're gonna expose the racket!
Oh, no! Please don't make me go talk to Mrs. Pynchbottom!!
Are you afraid of her because she owns this newspaper, and she can fire you?
No, I'm afraid of her because she's seven feet tall and she can punch me in the head with her sharp elbows!

Thank heaven! I was hoping you'd come!!
I knew you'd feel that way about it! Humid wasn't even sure this Fire Department scandal was big enough to bother you with! But I remembered how you always like to get involved in exposing corruption! So I said—
HOLD IT!! Lady, who are them guys?!?

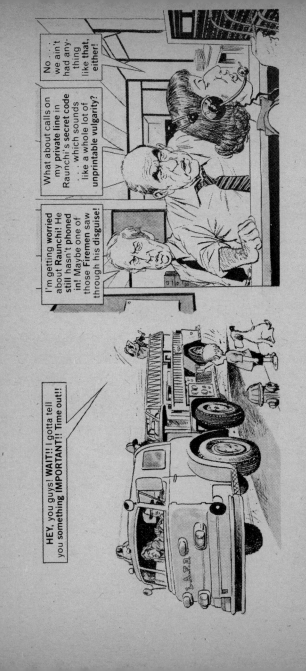

ONE EVENING IN AN OHIO BUS STATION

When a friend has a birthday, you send a birthday card. When a couple has an anniversary, you send an anniversary card. But there may be times when you won't be able to find the right card for the occasion. If this happens, we invite you to turn to this selection of

MAD

GREETING

CARDS

FOR VERY

SPECIAL

OCCASIONS

ARTIST: PAUL COKER   WRITER: FRANK JACOBS   WITH   EARLE DOUD

To a Would-Be Suicide

You cannot learn to tie a noose
        And pills stick in your throat;
You lack the skill to aim a gun;
        You try to drown—and float;
And so I guess it's up to me
        To supervise your fate;
This card's a rolled-up Navy raft;
        Just swallow—then inflate.

To A Pedigreed Dog Owner

It's clear to me how much you prize
    Your purebred female collie;
Two thousand bucks to buy a dog
    Is quite a sum, by golly!
I'd like to fill your life with joy,
    To lift your spirits, but—
Last weekend, when she was in heat,
    She made it with a mutt.

To an Auto Crash Victim

You have two badly broken arms;
    Your pelvis is a wreck;
Your head's in traction for a year
    From whiplash of the neck;
But though you'll suffer many months
    From wounds that will not heal,
Just look at it another way—
    Think how your car must feel.

TO AN EX-BOY FRIEND

What fun we had, the two of us,
  Those nights when we smoked pot,
Until that day you said, "Get lost!"
  And ditched me on the spot;
You treated me like so much dirt;
  I really was disgusted;
Which is my way of telling you
  Who went and got you busted.

TO AN EX-GIRLFRIEND

I love the park where first we met,
  The whisper of the breeze;
I love the grass where once we sat
  Beneath the noble trees;
I also love the wooden bench
  Where first we kissed and hugged;
They all remind me how I fled
  And left you to be mugged.

TO A HEALTH NUT

You don't eat fish or fowl or meat;
    You won't use salt or spices;
You've put a ban on cakes and pies,
    And eggs provoke a crisis;
This card's not meant to put you down;
    It's just an explanation
Why once again I'm passing up
    Your dinner invitation.

To A Confused Person

You comb the land from coast to coast,
    You search the whole wide earth,
In hopes some day that you will find
    A record of your birth;
And so I want to share with you
    What all your friends have known—
You'll never find the proof you seek,
    Because you are a clone.

To A Mass Murderer on Trial

You know the judge can send you up
    For your remaining years,
And so I send this card to you
    To banish all your fears;
No life in stir awaits you, pal;
    You won't be rotting there;
The Legislature's changed the law—
    They're bringing back the Chair.

AL'S ELECTRIC REPAIR

To A Terrorist

You victimize and kill and maim;
    In short, you go too far;
But nothing I can ever say
    Will change the way you are;
By now, whatever's left of you
    Lies scattered on the floor;
I bet you never opened up
    A letter-bomb before.

A MAD LOOK AT

TARZAN... TODAY

KEEP OFF THE TREES

Kenya Park Authority

ARTIST: JACK DAVIS   WRITER: DON EDWING

ENDANGERED
SPECIES

Coming Soon
CONGO
COOPERATIVE
APARTMENTS

TANZANIA

HYDRO-ELECTRIC
PROJECT #6

If a Doctor or a Dentist suggests surgery...or some type of expensive treatment...most people will make sure by getting a "Second Opinion."

"Second Opinions" however, can be very valuable in common everyday situations, too. So MAD recommends seeking them out. You'll see what we mean...with these examples of

SECOND OPINIONS IN NON- MEDICAL CASES

ARTIST: PAUL COKER
WRITER: DENNIS SNEE

If the Ticket Seller at a smash-hit
Broadway musical says. "Sold out!"...

..try looking for a Scalper in front
of the theater for a SECOND OPINION

...if your Dad tells you a College Education is a guaranteed ticket to a good job and a comfortable future...

...talk to any Grocery Clerk with a Master's Degree for a SECOND OPINION.

If your Teacher tells you that ours
is a nation of "Laws," not "Men"...

...talk to a member of the United Mine
Workers Union for a SECOND OPINION.

If "Zero Population Growth" advocates tell you that our declining birth rate is good news for the entire country...

...talk to any unemployed Elementary School Teacher for a SECOND OPINION.

If your Son's Piano Teacher tells you he has the potential to become another Van Cliburn...

...talk to your neighbors downstairs for a SECOND OPINION.

If your High School Guidance Counselor tells you that you have no future...

..see your nearest Army, Navy or Marine Recruiter for a SECOND OPINION.

If your Wife observes that the latest girl your son is dating seems to have absolutely nothing going for her...

...have one of those man-to-man talks with your Son for a SECOND OPINION.

If your new Girlfriend claims you're the first man she has ever loved...

...try a personal interview with her last Boyfriend for a SECOND OPINION.

If your History Teacher says the American Way has always been to show generosity toward her former adversaries after armed conflicts...

...talk to any American Indian around for a SECOND OPINION.

If your Bartender tells you that the Yankees can't possibly lose their next game with the Red Sox...

...talk to your Bookie for a SECOND OPINION.

If your Father tells you his childhood was one of bitter hardship and deprivation...

...talk "off-the-record" with your Grandmother for a SECOND OPINION.

ONE AFTERNOON DOWNTOWN ON MAIN STREET

THE LIGHTEF

NEIGH

I married the **girl next door!** We'd **started** going together as far back as **Elementary School!**

We were **Sweethearts** all the way through **Junior High School, High School** . . . and even **College!**

SIDE OF...
BORS

ARTIST & WRITER:
DAVE BERG

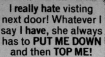

I really hate visting next door! Whatever I say I have, she always has to PUT ME DOWN and then TOP ME!

That's just her way of feeling important!

I really don't care WHAT her reasons are! It's downright ANNOYING!

So don't talk about anything GOOD!

Hi, Sam! Hi, Gladys! How are you?

To tell the truth, I'm not feeling well! I've had this terrible cold and it's gone to my chest! I'll probably end up with pneumonia . . . !

Big deal! Pneumonia!

I've had DOUBLE pneumonia!

Every night at **exactly eleven o'clock**, our **upstairs** neighbor goes to bed! First, he takes off one of his **heavy clodhopper** work shoes and drops it on the floor... like **THAT**!!

KLUMP!

Why aren't you going to **sleep**? And why are you **staring** up at the ceiling?

I can't go to sleep until the **other shoe** drops!

There! Okay! I'm **satisfied**! Now, I can go to sleep!

KLUMP!

KLUMP!

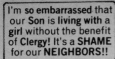

I'm so embarrassed that our **Son** is **living** with a **girl** without the benefit of **Clergy!** It's a **SHAME** for our **NEIGHBORS!!**

I can't **STAND** the idea that the people next door are **gloating** over our **troubles!**

Oh, **don't** be silly! Today, **ALL** parents are having problems!

Take the **McGillas** next door! Their **Daughter** just had a **BABY,** and she's **NOT MARRIED!**

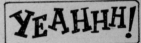

YEAHHH!

ONE MAGICAL DAY IN MODERN BAGHDAD

BOY ARE WE SICK AND TIRED OF MOVIES THAT TRY AND TELL US HOW MARVELOUS THINGS WERE BACK IN THE FIFTIES! ONCE AND FOR ALL, WE'D LIKE THEM TO....

ARTIST: MORT DRUCKER   WRITER: STAN HART

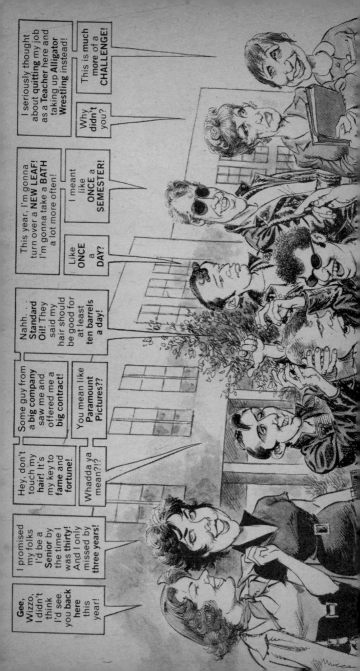

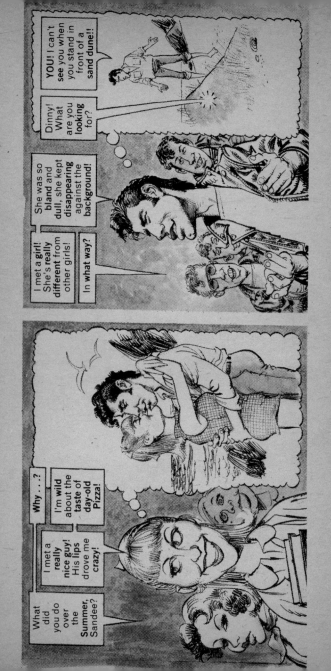

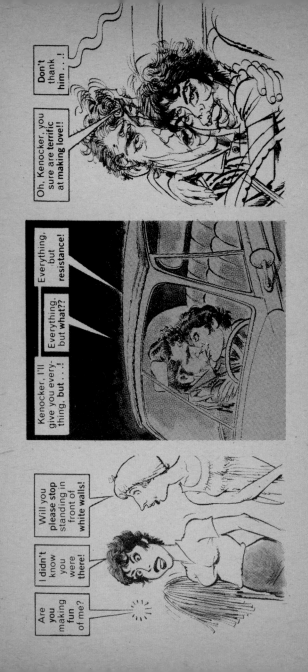

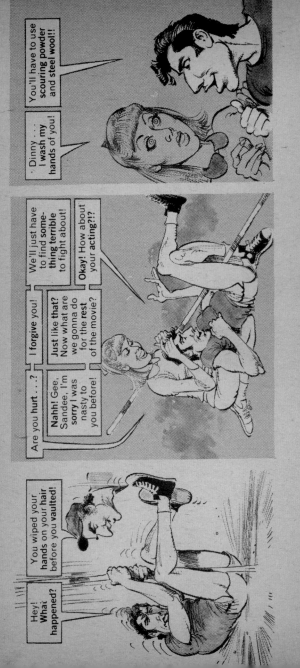

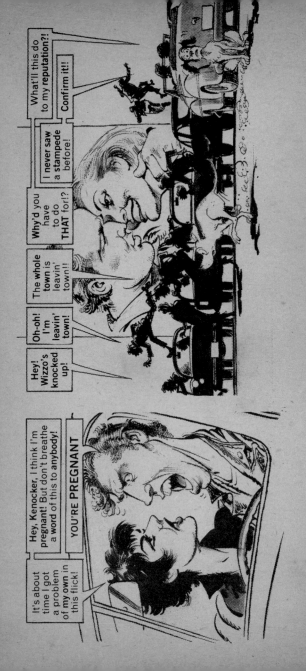

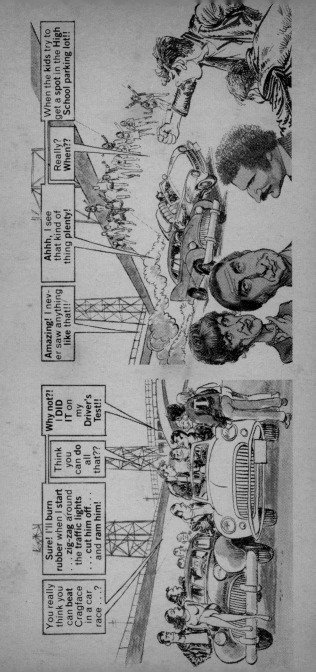

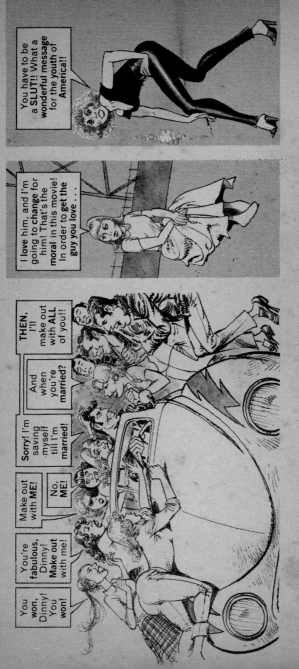